PUSHKIN PRE

The 19th-century boom in mass tourism, fuelled by the introduction of the railways, brought with it the rise of travel writing. Guided excursions such as "Cook's Tours" (the first of which was led by Thomas Cook in 1841, and went from Leicester to Loughborough) were not for everyone. Many preferred to strike out alone into the depths of foreign lands. Of these foreign lands, Norway appealed to the more intrepid: the grand scenery, exotic peasantry and comparative cheapness of the Far North suited the enthusiasm of the young (or female) tourist.

The books in "Found on the Shelves" have been chosen to give a fascinating insight into the treasures that can be found while browsing in The London Library. Now celebrating its 175th anniversary, with over seventeen miles of shelving and more than a million books, The London Library has become an unrivalled archive of the modes, manners and thoughts of each generation which has helped to form it.

From essays on dieting in the 1860s to instructions for gentlewomen on trout-fishing, from advice on the ill health caused by the "modern" craze of bicycling to travelogues from Norway, they are as readable and relevant today as they were more than a century ago— even if it is no longer the Norwegian custom for tourists to be awoken by "the best-looking girl in the house"!

# THE LURE
## *of the*
# NORTH

*The London Library*

*Pushkin Press*

Pushkin Press
71–75 Shelton Street,
London WC2H 9JQ

Extract from William Dawson Hooker, *Notes on Norway; or, A Brief
Journal of a Tour made to the Northern Parts of Norway in the Summer
of 1836*. Glasgow: Printed by Richardson, Hutchison & Co., 1837

Extracts from: *Unprotected Females in Norway; or, The Pleasantest
Way of Travelling There, passing through Denmark and Sweden, with
Scandinavian Sketches from Nature*, [by Miss E. Lowe] London: G.
Routledge & Co., 1857

*A Cruise on the Hardanger Fiord; or, Six in Norway with a "Snark"*,
by One of Them. Pamphlet reprinted from *The Field*, 13 August 1881

Map of Norway from Frederick Metcalfe, *The Oxonian in Norway;
or, Notes of Excursions in that Country*. 2nd edition, revised. London:
Hurst and Blackett, 1857

First published by Pushkin Press in 2016

9 8 7 6 5 4 3 2 1

ISBN 978 1 782272 48 9

Set in Goudy Modern by Tetragon, London

Printed by CPI Group (UK) Ltd, Croydon, CR0 4YY

www.pushkinpress.com

# NOTES ON NORWAY

*or,*
*A Brief Journal of a Tour made*
*to the Northern Parts of Norway*
*in the Summer of 1836*

## BY WILLIAM DAWSON HOOKER

WILLIAM DAWSON HOOKER was twenty when he travelled to Norway. In July 1836, he was a guest of the Crowe family in the most remote part of Norway. A medical student and the son of a prominent botanist (who would later become the first full-time director of the Royal Gardens at Kew), he was particularly interested in ornithology. Hooker published a dissertation on quinine before dying in Jamaica at the age of twenty-three.

*Laplanders at Kaafiord*

**S**unday, 31st.—After breakfast, Mr. Crowe's house was thrown open to all the English in Kaafiord, who soon filled the room to hear divine service; and Mrs. Crowe, who was, by this time, "as well as could be expected," made her appearance. This lady is a native of the country and considered one of the belles of the North of Norway. De Capell Brooke's likeness of her is far from doing justice to her fine complexion, beautiful light hair, and charming features.

The Sunday is here considered to be over at six in the afternoon. The storehouse is then open, and it is the busiest time in the whole week, for as the hours are not counted as working ones, so the people almost all make a point of getting *pisk* or drunk on the Sabbath. The Mountain Lapps generally come down on that day with their Deer, from their summer encampments or *Rehu-bye*, to attend church, and afterwards make purchases and become intoxicated. I took this opportunity of sketching the particular dresses of these people; they did not like at first to be made the subject of a drawing; the cause of this originates in a superstitious idea, which is pretty common among the ignorant, that having the likeness of any person gives the possessor a power of bringing harm upon the individual whose likeness it is. This was of course the true reason why one man refused, though I was much amused at the objections he started, when I expressed a wish to sketch his wife, a mountain Lapp, who was a remarkably characteristic specimen of her national peculiarities. "No," said the husband, "it must not be: she has not her gold and silver ornaments on." After a while, however, and what was of more effect than the persuasions of Mr. Woodfall, after a few glasses of rum, he consented; and when I showed him her likeness and costume, he exclaimed, "that it was as like as if looking into a looking-glass;" and he was particularly delighted at hearing that my drawing was going to England, where it would be shown as his beautiful consort. The man was already very proud of her, and this circumstance raised her value at least fifty per cent. in his eyes.

An occurrence took place here this evening, as it does every Sunday, which I was very desirous of witnessing, and this was a Quān dance. It was held in a house close by; and having persuaded Captain Thomas to go also, we proceeded thither. No dressing indeed was required; thick boots and a pea-jacket were my equipment; and all the instructions I received were, to carry plenty of tobacco. So, pipe in mouth, I sallied forth, through mud, wet and rain, walking into the apartment without a whit of introduction, and there I already found the *Harriet's* Skipper, skipping round the room with a Quān damsel, whose flat and shapeless face was aptly compared to a model in putty, which had been sate upon before it had hardened. We squeezed our way up to the top of the room, where there was a large fire, over which five or six old women were cowering, one of whom busied herself in stroking a child's head, and ever and anon committing to the exterminating flames some unlucky straggler which she found there. The men had, almost all, birch pipes in their mouths, and these they did not always relinquish while dancing. Fearing to give mortal offence if I departed without joining in the evening's amusement (I do not mean the ancient crone's occupation), I looked round for the most cleanly girl in the room, and began waltzing till I could hardly stop myself, being regaled the while with delectable odours of salt-fish and ill-prepared deer-skins. I was astonished to see both men and women swallowing large draughts of cold water, while in a state of profuse perspiration, and seeming to receive no injury from a practice which would give most Englishmen inflammation in the bowels, or something of the kind. These poor creatures were certainly more innocently employed than their neighbours at the store, not a drop of spirits being touched among them. We had not been long in the house when we were summoned back to Mr. Crowe's, where the ladies had got up a dance and were in want of partners, and these companions being far more agreeable than the Quān belles, and the mode of dancing less violent, we kept up the festivity till far into morning, and went to bed sufficiently tired.

Monday, August, 1st.——A party was formed to see the mines, and I started with them, but soon proved a deserter, being anxious to sketch the environs of Kaafiord, the Bay, Works, &c. during which time my friends having completed their subterranean researches, emerged from the bowels of the earth, the ladies having a most picturesque appearance in the miners' caps and cloaks. I then rejoined them, and we returned home.

Just at this time our French acquaintances arrived, having accomplished their excursion to the North Cape, and being desirous of visiting the copper mines and works at Kaafiord, whither they immediately proceeded, and were highly pleased, especially with the process of purifying the copper, as performed in the laboratory of Captain Thomas. They

*Entrance of Kaafiord*

afterwards dined at Mr. Crowe's hospitable board, and spoke of Bossikop, which they had been visiting, and whither some of our party had already gone. I followed shortly after, in company with my kind friend, Captain Thomas, having persuaded Mr. Walker to come also. From Kaafiord to Bossikop is about ten miles by water, and the people seldom think of travelling, in summer, by any other means. We therefore got into a native boat, one of the Norway yauls, and a more comfort-able conveyance can hardly be imagined. I shall endeavour to describe these vessels. They are very light, and at the same time, particularly strong, not difficult of management, nor easily upset; they carry a large square sail in the very middle of the boat, the stern sheets are also large and without any after-thorts. The tim-bers are so tightly put together that not a drop of water ever makes its way in. When used for short excursions, Reindeer-skins are laid in the bottom of the boat, and the traveller rolls himself up in his *Paesk*, and puts on his *Skall-komāgers*, while the heap of baggage,

similarly enveloped, serves for a pillow, and he
has another Deer-skin above him. Thus, nothing can be more comfortable than such a *gîte*.
The tiller, which one might suppose would
be in the way, is quite differently contrived;
at first it projects, over the side, and then,
with a joint, it turns along the gunwale, and
is held by the man who manages the sail and
sternmost oar. He sits looking *forward*, and
rowing one oar, while others handle two oars,
and sit looking *aft*. Accidents seldom happen,
unless the men be *pisk*. The fellows are clever,
and their craft both sail and pull fast. The
thole pins are curious contrivances: to make
these, the boat builder selects a crooked birch
branch, and fixes it to the side of the boat,
with one of the limbs of the branch sticking
above the gunwale, and pointing aft; the oar
is tied to this, and works underneath it, thus
obviating the necessity of removing it when
the rower requires to use his hand for something else. The oar is short, light, and more
paddle-shaped than ours. The boats are turned
up at both ends, about four breadths of planks

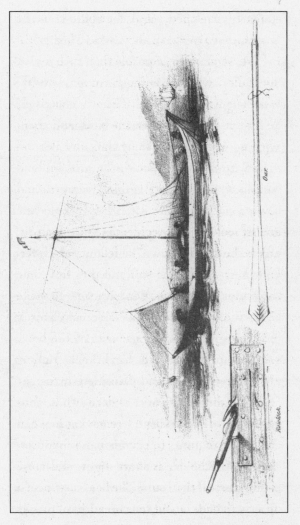

*Oar.*

*Rowlock.*

*Norwegian yaul*

sufficing for them, and these are fastened together by wooden pins, instead of nails.

We slept very comfortably, till roused by the boat thumping against Mr. Vendal's wooden pier, at Bossikop. This was about half-past two, a.m. No one was to be seen, but proceeding to the house of Madame Klerck, we found it unlocked, though the inmates were all in bed, and asleep. Captain Thomas went to rouse some slumberer, who should get our beds ready, and our hostess, as soon as she heard of our arrival, sent down wine and cake, after partaking of which, we retired to finish our night's rest on shore. Madame Klerck is the widow of a highly respectable merchant at Bossikop. The regulation in this country is that, in order to secure the exclusive right of carrying on mercantile transactions in any district, the individual must become a *Giestgiver*, that is, must entertain all strangers at a certain fixed rate; this rate is, of course, much too low to repay the trouble and expense to which they are subjected, and is therefore a kind of tax for their privilege; and Madame Klerck, though she *let* the business to the hands of another, is compelled, either by her own hospitable feelings, or by law, to continue the custom, which she does indeed with the greatest possible kindness. The couches we went to, were quite novel to us; the beds and pillows being of *Eider down*, and the coverlids stuffed with the same material. This latter article was at once warm and light, but we sunk so deeply into our beds, that one of the party likened them to the Potter's field—places to "bury strangers in."

Tuesday, August 2nd.——We were roused this morning from our *downy* slumbers, by the entrance of a damsel, who offered to each of us a cup of strong coffee to sip in bed; not as a substitute for breakfast, but simply to serve as an awakening draught and to rouse us thoroughly. This custom we found to be universal in all Norske families; my father had witnessed it in Iceland; and as was the case there, so here the best-looking girl in the house is selected to perform this office. It is certainly not unpleasant to see a fair-haired blue-eyed child of the north, the first thing in the morning, before one is fairly awake, and to sip the refreshing coffee, which is proffered with such modest grace, as induced some of us to doze a little longer, in hopes of being favoured with a second visit. Having leaped from our couches and commenced dressing, we, who were strangers, felt not a little abashed at seeing our Hebe return for our empty cups before we were half clad, and wished ourselves back in bed; but she walked quite unconcernedly past us, reminding me forcibly of the scripture expression, "thinking no evil," for it seemed to be a matter of no moment to her whether we were dressed or not; and when we said, "mony tak," she quietly curtsied, and replied, "welbekommen," and went away with our cups.

Madame Klerck was waiting for us when we came down, and cordially welcomed us to Bossikop. I recognised her as one of Mr. Crowe's late guests, whose name, as well as that of many others, had escaped my memory, or defied the powers of my tongue, albeit habituated to

Scottish appellations, to pronounce, while at the same time, the appearance of the individual's person was faithfully retained.

Our French friends had also come down, and we all seated ourselves to a *"Frököst"* (breakfast) which was of a pretty substantial nature, and then, taking our guns, accompanied M. Le Baron Sibouet to visit the Ripas copper mines, situated upon the mountains of the same name. Our course lay over a most beautiful and level tract of country, cutting through a portion of the great Alten forest, till we came to an open plain of several miles in extent, clothed with tufts of *Vaccinium Myrtillus*, the *Blaebaer*, (in Scots, *Blaeberry*) and of *Kräkebaer* (*Crowberry*), among which were immense numbers of ant-hills, formed of the twigs and small leaves of the latter. The formic acid smelt quite strong, and I was afterwards told by a native of Sweden, that in the central parts of that country they often boil these ants, and, straining the liquor, obtain a kind of weak vinegar. The soil here was light and sandy, and seemed to be all of an alluvial character. We saw several beautiful *Peregrine Falcons*, but these birds kept a true "hawk's eye" upon us, so after a fruitless chase of an hour or more, we continued our way, and soon reached the noble Alten river, a broad, deep, and rapid stream, which is continually under-mining its banks, and increasing the size of its channel. My most sanguine expectations were surpassed by the loveliness of the scenery. I sat down to attempt a delineation of its highly picturesque beauties, but the more I tried, the further did I feel from attaining my object; for, after finishing my sketch, and comparing it with the lovely original, I felt utterly disheart-ened at observing how it failed in conveying the least idea of the brilliant and living reality. On this side of the river, I mean about the spot where I sat, there were no mosquitoes; for what reason I could not tell; but one or two places were equally exempt, and I vainly puz-zled my brains to account for the circumstance of the absence of these plagues: no difference being apparent, except that the localities in question are invariably and pre-eminently the most beautiful I ever saw. The native name for Mosquito is *Mouga* or *Mouge*, an appellation as like the Scottish word Midge as is the insect's propensity for human blood. Nor are the natives of Norway themselves by any means exempt from the attacks of these persevering phlebotomizers. I remember to have seen one countryman perfectly blinded for a time; I prescribed for him Goulard water, with excellent effect. The mention of mosquitoes calls to mind the *Furia infernalis*, of which both Linnaeus and Dr. Clarke speak; but their horrifying tales are quite scouted by the Norwegians, who attach no credit to either of these eminent Naturalists' relations.

We were ferried across the Alten in long canoes, one man standing on the bow, and another on the stern, and punting us over, while we lay huddled together at the bottom of the boat. We passed a number of stakes or posts, stretched across a ford on the river; one post was set upright, while another was laid obliquely on the top, with its lower end driven into the bed of the stream; upon these piles the people set their salmon nets, but in what manner I could not learn. As soon as we had reached the other side the *Mougas* attacked us with renewed vigour, and our guide was sadly annoyed with them. This man, a Russian by birth, had been too long absent from his native country to be able to speak its language perfectly, and he was even more deficient in every other; a very little Norske and Russ, some Quānish, and about twenty words of English, completed the vocabulary in which poor Prakopen gave vent to all his wrath against the mosquitoes; and truly ludicrous was the jargon he uttered, at which all our own sufferings could not hinder us from laughing immoderately. This fellow had married a Quān woman, of whose beauty he was so proud that he took me one day to see her. I could not resist the temptation of joking with him, and telling Prakopen, whose eyes sparkled with pride, that his spouse was more resplendent than the sun, and more lovely than the moon; but to speak plainly, she was just like her countrywomen, detestably ugly.

In this part of Norway, an excellent plan is adopted for carrying luggage and loose articles; they are deposited in a kind of flat square basket, formed of thin slips of Fir wood, light and yet strong; cords, which pass over and under each shoulder, attach this basket pretty firmly to the back, much after the fashion of a soldier's knapsack, thus the arms are left free and unencumbered, by which the bearer is enabled to assist himself in climbing the hills, &c.

After shooting a number of Ducks and Flappers in the marshes, we proceeded up the Ripas mountains to the mines. These mines, which are but recently opened, and belong to the Alten Company, are peculiarly rich, the ore yielding a much larger per centage of metal than those at Kaafiord.

We rested in a *Gamme*, or Lapp hut, and I no longer wondered at the prevalence of sore eyes among the lower classes—a circumstance which I had, previously, chiefly attributed to the winter's snows dazzling them,—the hut being so full of smoke that I could hardly breathe. The roofs of the Ripas mines are very low, so that, though stooping considerably, I still received some contusions on my head. In these mines there are some *shafts* which descend a considerable depth. I found pretty specimens of red arseniate of Cobalt, and of green carbonate of Copper, or Malachite. After exploring the mines we returned to the River, and observed Prakopen issuing from the ferry house and eating raw Salmon. He offered me some, assuring me that it was quite freshly caught, and *meiget gut*. This fish is called *Lax* here, as in Iceland, and I should have cheerfully tried how it tasted uncooked and uncured, but that I could not resolve to eat it after it had been fingered over by a filthy Russ. Glad were we to obtain a temporary respite from the mosquitoes; M. Le Baron exclaiming, "à bas les Moustiches," Prakopen denouncing them as emissaries of *Gamle Eric* (Old Nick,) and we all wishing that they were like the Egyptian locusts, laid in the depths of the Red Sea.

The *Pedicularis Sceptrum Caroli* was abundant in this vicinity, growing in similar localities to those where I had first seen this interesting plant; there were also a great variety of *Willows*, which I gathered, hoping they would find a place in the rich Salicetum of His Grace the Duke of Bedford, binding up their ends in moss to keep them moist, till Mr. Christy should see them, and determine whether they were worth the conveyance home. I also collected such ripe seeds of different Willows and other plants as I could find, pocketing, doubtless, in my ignorance, much trash and plenty of duplicates. A few *Alders* grew in moist places, and abundance of *Wild Currants*, very sour and bad, and infested with a dusty red blight, similar to what attacks our Gooseberry, only more powdery.

When we reached Bossikop, we found that a number of Ladies had arrived, together with Mr. Crowe, Mr. Christy, the Bergmaster, Mr. Galt, our Captain, and Dr. Greisdale. Our party, however, dined alone, and I was not sorry that we did so, as I should have been utterly ashamed to let any one see the inordinate appetites we displayed, and the consequent clearance of provisions that we made.

On adjourning to the withdrawing room, I found Frue Grüntwyt, Yungfrue Stabell, and the *Amptmaninde*, or Amptman's lady, singing Norske songs to the accompaniment of the piano-forte. They displayed great taste and feeling in their performance, and many of the airs were very pleasing, especially that mentioned by Dr. Clarke, of which the words begin:

For Norge Kiempers Föde land,
Vi denne Skaal udtomme.

I had thought that in these hyperborean latitudes the art of music would have been neglected, so that it was quite an agreeable surprize to me to find that both here and at Hammerfest there is a great deal of taste displayed for this delightful amusement. Some of the old national strains appear quite to inspire the people, and even a stranger (I, at least) could not hear them unmoved. The Lapps do not sing, except a kind of howling incantation which they chant against the Wolves, be so termed; four or five words uttered incessantly, at the very top of their voice, till the lungs are collapsed for want of air, compose all the music with which these people are acquainted.

The Fins or Quāns, again, sing, and are rather musical in their way; and the Russian sailors were continually exercising their voices, especially in the evenings; at such times, when many of these people joined in the strain,

> "The sounds, by distance tame,
> "Mellowed along the waters came,
> "And lingering long by *Fiord* and Bay,
> "Wailed every harsher note away."

I have often stood and listened with pleasure, under such circumstances, to lays which would perhaps have proved harsh and monotonous if they had sounded close upon the ear. Thus

> "distance lends enchantment"

to sound as well as to sight.

August 3rd, Wednesday.—A party were again proceeding to the Ripas mines, but

unwilling to be quite demolished by the mosquitoes, and thinking I might spend my time
more agreeably in the pursuit of Birds and fine
scenery, I declined accompanying them, and
set off in an opposite direction, first, however, going to visit a poor woodcutter who had
wounded his leg with a hatchet. Mr. Walker
accompanied me, but previously we found
it needful to obtain an interpreter (*taalk*)
who should also serve as a guide (*wappus*). A
Swede, who had been some time in England,
and spoke our language very fluently, offered
his services, and among other things he com-
municated to us his regrets that he had been
so foolish as to marry a Norske woman, by
whom he had several children, and was thus
prevented by law from returning to England,
where he wished he could settle, as he felt
confident he could soon make his fortune! I
found my patient had received a severe cut,
the bone having been chipped. Upon enquiring
what application had been used, the people
showed me a substance which they procure by
boiling the young tops of Fir, sliced into small

pieces, thus extracting the juice, and making, in fact, *Riga Balsam*. No one had given them any directions how to prepare or apply this substance; "but," said they, "our forefathers always used it, and so do we." This little discovery in Pharmaceutics quite pleased me, and with the freely proffered milk, dried salmon, and Rye cake, together with the sincere and still more acceptable "mony tak," I thought myself well repaid for the expense of a guide, and a few miles' walk.

Acerbi, I find, has noticed this Norwegian mode of dressing wounds; when at Alten he searched the empty dwelling of a Lapp family, "and found nothing," he says, "in the way of curiosity, but a box of Rosin: this juice issues from the Fir tree, and the Laplanders make an ointment of it for dressing wounds."

The house of my patient was situated on the banks of the Alten river, just at a spot where the stream undermines its banks, and carries away every year three or four yards of soil, depositing as much sand on the opposite side. Our guide was a very shrewd and intelligent fellow. To my enquiries about the *Capercailzie* (*Tetrao urogallus*) he replied that the cock bird of this species is comparatively scarce now in the neighbourhood, and not known by that name at all, but is called *Stor Fügle*, the "big bird," par excellence; while the hen, which is far more common, goes by the name of *Tioure*. Wolves are also comparatively rare, not being seen in droves, but only one or two at a time; and Bears hardly show themselves in summer, so that our hopes of an encounter with Bruin were quite disappointed, whom the natives call *Björn*.

Mr. Walker having proceeded to the other side of the river, in order to entomologize, I seated myself on the bank of the Alten, to make a sketch of the surrounding scenery; when, all of a sudden, the earth on which I was sitting gave way, and with a couple of as complete somersets as were ever flung at Astley's amphitheatre, I was precipitated into the stream, where, had I been unable to swim, I should have met with a very cold-water grave. "Facilis descensus," thought I, as my sketch-book, containing all my previous journal, notes, and most of my drawings, &c., went gallantly sailing down to the Fiord, whither, feeling no inclination to follow it, I struck out my arms and legs, using my utmost endeavours to extricate myself from this icy bath, well knowing that my most powerful exertions were not more than sufficient to carry me, encumbered as I was with all my clothes, komager-boots and a well filled shot-belt, across a broad, deep, and rapid river. At last I emerged, but at the bank opposite to that from which I had entered. To have ascended the latter, would, indeed, have been impossible, as the bank dipped abruptly from a height of twenty feet into the river. The dog, Lion by name, who had plunged boldly into the river after me, was no where to be seen, and I began to feel much at a loss what to do, for the idea of returning by the way I came was by no means agreeable; moreover, the mosquitoes, now that I was on this side of the river, began to torment me desperately; my tinder was wet, as well as my powder, so I could not smoke. After a while I espied a countryman, and requested him to ferry me across, but whether from unwillingness, or from ignorance of the meaning of my broken Norske, he continually replied, "Nae, nae," though I backed my eloquence with the persuasive argument of a wet and ragged twenty-four skilling note, which I extracted from my soaked pocket, and gave him to understand that it should become his if he complied with my request. Finding that no help could be obtained from that quarter, I set to running up the river in search of Mr. Walker, when to my great joy I espied Prakopen trudging along loaded with the provision basket which belonged to the Ripas party. However, the rights of property weighed with me but little, under my present shivering and half-drowned circumstances; and first the *schnapps* and the eatables suffered considerable diminution, which was increased when Mr. Walker arrived. After being thus re-invigorated, Mr. Walker and I recrossed the Alten's frigid waters, and to my great satisfaction I found my gun lying safely where I left it, and Lion sitting beside it.

The party from the Ripas mines had arrived at Bossikop before us, and were proceeding to supper at the Fogedgaard, with the widow of the late Foged. As soon as I had changed my wet garments, I followed them, and found a large number of persons assembled; but as Captain Moyse was going to send to Kaafiord that night, I accompanied the boat, wishing to obtain from on board the *Harriet*, some more drawing paper, powder and shot, &c. I therefore wrapped myself again in my paesk, and lying down in the bottom of the boat, soon reached our good ship, where, after executing my own errands, and the commissions of my friends, I passed the rest of the night.

SKETCH MAP

OF

**NORWAY.**

*English Miles*
10 20 30 40 50      100      120

NORTHERN   OCEAN

North Cape
Porsanger Ferd
Laxe Ferd
Maaso Ferd
Varangra Fd.

Lofføden Isles

RUSSIAN
LAPLAND

Arctic Circle

Helgeland Isles

Lulea
Pitea
Tornea
Uleaborg

Folden Fjord

GULF   OF   BOTHNIA

FINLAND

Umea

Trondjem

Ostersund

Rasa
Christine-stad

Bergen

Gefle

GULF OF FINLAND
Revel

Stavanger

CHRISTIANIA
Carlstad
Orebro

Upsala
Westeras
STOCKHOLM

Abo

Dago

Christiansand

Nykoping

# UNPROTECTED FEMALES IN NORWAY

*or,*

*The Pleasantest Way of Travelling There,*
*passing through Denmark and Sweden,*
*with Scandinavian Sketches from Nature*

BY MISS E. LOWE, 1857

Although this book was published anonymously, the "unprotected females" in question are known to be EMMELINE LOWE and her mother. These intrepid travellers would go on to publish *Unprotected females in Sicily, Calabria and on Top of Mount Aetna,* before giving up such independent adventures when Emmeline Lowe was married in 1859.

*Invitation to Norway—Incumbrances
left at Home—Best Route*

To the real traveller an unexplored country has the most enticing charms; but where is such a country to be found—where? A distant voice answers—*Here*. The little word comes from the Dovre-fjeld in the middle of Norway, and travels more than 1,000 miles ere it reach us: but distance does not lessen its truthful sound; and, confiding in that simple promise, we prepare to leave for the wildest part of Scandinavia. If, reader, you also like an unsophisticated country, inhabited by a fine race of upright peasantry, who will receive you as a guest, not cheat you as a traveller, prepare to follow us bodily, sharing our hardships and our pleasures, first laying in an immense stock of health, spirits, and good temper;—but should you be wanting in any of these, merely follow us in imagination, and from a comfortable fire-side chair, indulgently participate in what we shall endeavour to describe, without the trouble of travelling.

Very few have any idea what a country Norway is to attack, and the consequences of going off the high road at all. Christiania is 990 miles from London, and that is only the beginning of the real journey; new modes of conveyance, a new language, and scanty living, are all to come; and when a traveller has been sleeping on hay, ironing his own clothes, and had nothing but porridge three times a day for a week, if his spirits, health, and temper hold out, he has a real good supply of them, and is a "bonâ fide" traveller. To him the grand and rare sight of nature and human nature both combined and pure in their highest aspect, will alleviate any temporary hardship, which he must remember millions of his fellow-creatures suffer compulsorily every day of their lives, without any compensation. We two ladies, having gone before, show how practicable the journey must be, though we have found out and will maintain that ladies *alone* get on in travelling much better than with gentlemen: they set about things in a quieter manner, and always have their own way; while men are sure

to go into passions and make rows, if things are
not right immediately. Should ladies have no
escort with them, then every one is so civil, and
trying of what use they can be; while, when
there is a gentleman of the party, no one thinks
of interfering, but all take it for granted they
are well provided for.

The only use of a gentleman in travelling is
to look after the luggage, and we take care to
have no luggage. "The Unprotected" should
never go beyond one portable carpet-bag. This,
if properly managed, will contain a complete
change of everything; and what is the use of
more in a country where dress and finery
would be in the worst taste? Two waterproof
bags, with straps, and no key (a thing always
missing), straw hats which will not blow up,
thin mosquito veils, solid plaid shirts with
light polkas, woollen stockings, and hobnail
shoes, are the proper Norwegian accoutre-
ments, with a light hooded waterproof cloak
to go over all, much the same as would be taken
for a Highland tour, with the addition of two
other things; a driving-whip and fishing-rod;

the former is generally represented by a switch at the Norwegian posting-houses, and it is the greatest resource in the world to have the latter to throw into the nearest stream, without fear of a loud "Holloa!" if kept waiting for, or in want of, a meal.

Thus equipped, leaving crochet and scandal to the watering-places, we set off by express train from London one fine morning in July, and found ourselves, *viâ* Calais, at eight o'clock in the evening in Ghent, without any particular adventure, except a shower of rain penetrating the Belgian railway-carriage, obliging passengers to hold up umbrellas, which no doubt explained the reason of the comfortable old Flemish lady waiting at Malines, having one in each hand. The next day's journey took us to Aix-la-Chapelle, and the third to Hanover, when we rested for Sunday, there being English service at the Embassy, and on Monday afternoon were in Hamburg. There are several other ways of reaching Norway; this is the comfortable one. The economical plan is to sail direct from

Hull to Christiania—a three-days voyage, and
nothing of the coast seen; but as that is one of
the grandest features of the rugged North, I
should not recommend missing it.

\* \* \*

On the little steamer reaching Elstad, we
were 144 miles up the country, transported
entirely by public conveyances, whose exist-
ence is kept a profound secret in the capital, a
profitable trade being carried on there by the
selling and hiring of carrioles to travellers,
under the impression that they will not find
them on the roads. Every post-house between
Christiania and Trondhjem is plentifully sup-
plied with them, and unless a traveller intend
coming every year to Norway, and going as far
north as Hammerfest at least, I do not recommend his troubling himself with one of his
own, and being liable to all the accidents that
may happen to it and the harness. Most of the
English regretted having encumbered themselves with one, particularly on the long water
stages, where the unwheeling for embarking

and disembarking is a most serious business;
and many had sent them round by the steamer,
in company with the portmanteau containing
the clothes which they said were intended to
make them look "respectable on Sundays." It
used to amuse us so, every one having a trunk
somewhere, which always contained just the
thing they wanted, instead of resolving man-
fully to separate from luggage and England
together, not letting it tour about the country
like Madeira wine going to India and back to
be improved. On landing from the steamer, all
connection with the public ceased,—we were
to be thrown on our own resources. The captain, who spoke English, accompanied us on to
the end of the little pier, where we found waiting a pretty light carriage on springs, with
red body and green wheels, which held two
people. The bags were put in behind; a smart
boy in a scarlet cap jumped up with them, a
little cream-coloured cob trotted off, the captain waved his hand, and there we were left
with the boy and pony, and Norway before us.

*Left to our own resources—A Norwegian Station—A Landlord and a Goose—Gallantry*

We got on splendidly. The pony ran briskly along the Golden Valley, uphill and downhill at equal pace, requiring no whip; the red-capped boy gaily waved the reins over our heads. The springs of the carriage were easy; the road, though undulating, of smooth quality; and altogether those ten miles seemed wonderfully short, when we approached what the Norwegians call a "station" or spot for changing horses. I had fancied it to be a place resembling a busy inn-yard; and having heard a great deal about the postmasters, thought they were persons in official uniform, always on the watch for travellers, and who spoke a language or two; instead of which some solitary farm-buildings, tenanted by two women, who did nothing but stare, did not promise much chance of expeditious forwarding. As this was a "fast" station (one where

43

horses should be in readiness), I must confess to having been rather cross at the aspect of things, which I much regretted afterwards, and hope no English will be so in future; for when the women were fairly stirred up, they ran off for the postmaster, a rough peasant at work in the fields, and he instantly fitted out two first-rate carrioles, the women keeping up our spirits with brandiviin and cream; and when two honest farmers cheerfully left their ploughing to accompany us, we felt that deep confidence in the people established, which never for a moment forsook us during the whole of our journey; and which would have made us follow a Norwegian guide round the world, had he said he knew the way.

The carrioles were a variety, and are considered more dashing than the other little conveyances, which are sometimes quizzed as carts, but they were really much easier to sit in; carrioles (which the peasants, however wealthy, seldom use) having greater movement; and when there are only two people, it is more interesting sitting together, and noticing the thousand novel objects in a new country, instead of bawling to each other along the road. The same umbrella and the same coverings do for both, and, if there be any scarcity of animals, the same horse, which can be pulled up for the traveller to admire some lovely cascade or view, without his companion going on out of sight. The carrioles are used by the travelling natives for greater speed, and by the English for the same reason. But let those who want real enjoyment, and are content to see Norway at the rate of six miles an hour, always ask for a "*reise kjerre,*" pronounced *rysa kerria*.

My peasant was most chatty. After a great deal of talk, very difficult to follow, and which luckily seemed to require no answer, the word "Palmerston" was brought out most emphatically, with an authoritative query whether "*that* were not a fine man?" "Oh! a splendid fellow," was the reply, which gave unbounded satisfaction, and showed the advantage of having ready-learned a few Norwegian superlatives. A great deal more followed upon British politics, which sounded rather confused in the party arrangements, but had a liberal tendency altogether; and I found saying *Ja* (Yes) after every question was quite sufficient to keep up conversation, and prevented the usual political wind-up of a quarrel. It was extraordinary how this *Ja* satisfied the peasants on all points, and was a great deal better than saying nothing. Two Englishmen passed, who were going to embark in the returning steamer, accompanied by several Norwegian ponies they were taking out of the country. Before being told their nationality, it was quite easy to find it out, by their not bowing to other travellers, which gives a dullness to meeting on such solitary roads, and looks sulky. Why can they not imitate the pleasing customs of a nation, and take some little hints about things which make a pleasant moment in life, instead (as is too often the case) catching up the unfavourable ways of foreigners, such as excessive smoking, &c.?

Driving into the midst of a number of detached buildings, the political peasant declared them the roosting quarters for the night, if we were wise, which we were, in taking his advice; and after payment, he drove off home, to con his newspaper for the rest of the evening. Now, as to payment, that is the easiest thing possible; and though only at the second station, I was quite perfect in it already, from the beautiful simplicity (quite equal to that of the Three-per-Cents) of the arrangements. This is the way to proceed:—

Buy a small blue book, published by government in Christiania; open it as if you understood Norwegian thoroughly; the distance from station to station on every high-road in the country is marked in order; look for that you are on; then turn to the table of prices for horses, carrioles, &c., at the beginning; pay with an authoritative air, as if accustomed to travel; add four skillings extra for the peasant himself, and your hand will be seized, shaken, and the emphatic word "*Tak*" pronounced, evidently the original of the fashionable modern abomination "Thanks."

The charges for posting are—for a single horse from a "slow" station (that is, one where they are not kept in readiness), twenty-four skillings per Norske mile: from fast stations in the country, and slow ones in towns, thirty-six skillings: and from fast ones in towns, forty-eight skillings; the carriole or car, with the harness, are six skillings per mile extra; saddles, three skillings. At all slow stations the postmaster is entitled to four skillings for the trouble of ordering each horse. For two people travelling in the same vehicle with one horse, an animal and a half is charged. Sending a messenger on before to order horses is called "forbud," and is paid at the rate of one horse. Comparing these prices with the exchange for English money, will at once show how reasonably the luxury of driving good animals can be had in Norway. Should the peasant be particularly cross (an impossibility), he must not have anything extra for himself. If you happen to be really in a hurry to get on, and he objects to fast driving, make him get into the carriole himself, while you jump up behind; the change of attitude is delightful, and so bewildering to him, that he will allow you to go at any rate you like. The little government blue book, published every month at Christiania, contains all particulars about distances; the peasants never seem inclined to dispute any point, taking, when they do not understand what the amount ought to be, the traveller's word for it.

The innumerable buildings of which a station is composed made it puzzling to know which to enter; a Norwegian lady, who was waiting, came forward, and pointed out the kitchen department, where the mistress was busy; another where the meals were eaten; and quite a choice of log huts with beds. Securing a couple, and ordering supper, we proposed walking with the lady into the village: she, astonished, said, "What village?" Such a thing was unknown in this part of the country; only station farms, and here and there a church, being met with the whole way to Trondhjem, nearly 200 miles off. The church of Quam was in the vicinity; where Colonel Sinclair lies; that gallant Scotchman who, in 1612, tried, with nine hundred followers, to cut his way through Norway, to help Gustavus Adolphus in Sweden, and of course was cut off himself instead. He must have been dreadfully hard up, or else would not have parted with his national prudence. His enemy's descendants have erected, in remembrance of the combat, a small wooden cross, in a care of the rock on the road-side, twelve miles further up the valley. The young Norwegian lady, who spoke a little English, regretted her "darling" was not with her, meaning her husband.

The supper of fresh salmon and coffee was excellent, though eaten in the presence of a circle of spectators, who looked on in the most innocent manner at the English ladies, occasionally whispering, *pynt, megget pynt*; which expression, fair reader, should you be at all good-looking (and if British or American you must be so, the proportion of ugliness to either being one in a million), you will hear every five minutes in Norway. The people have no idea of concealing their opinions; and, as long as they are of so pleasing a nature, you need not be angry. Another of their ejaculations is much more trying, and I feel in duty bound to mention it, that those ladies who have an objection to revelations or telling fibs may keep out of the country. It is no less than the query, "How old are you?" Every person we spoke to, all the peasants we had anything to do with, in the midst of the greatest haste, before starting on the longest expedition, it was first solemnly asked; and when satisfied as to my advance on the journey of life, next came "How old is your mamma?" The reply to that question having been always shrouded in mystery to me, I could fairly answer "I did not know," which made them shrug their shoulders, as if my education had been sadly neglected.

Our public supper over, a ladder led to the very comfortable beds, from which we were roused next morning by the water for wash-ing arriving in a slop-bowl. After sending the good-natured, moon-faced maiden to refill it twenty times; breakfasting very tolerably, and shaking an unlimited number of hands; a succession of little cream-coloured cobs, changed at every station, bore us through the valley, whose character became wilder and more Tyrolese each moment. The constant cascades formed the most charming road-side variety; any one of them would have made the fortune of an English watering-place; and there they were tumbling refreshingly down, quite grateful for being sketched. Halting for lunch at Laurgaard, a plateful of rice-porridge was brought, which, with cream and wild strawberries, made a delicious summer meal. Continuing on, enjoying the driving, and laughing at the ludicrous harness of the ponies, which consisted chiefly of an article on each side of the neck like a flat-iron, which jogged up and down in the most fidgety manner, I dropped the whip, and looking behind, to tell the boy to pick it up, found the urchin had disappeared completely, having slily run back, finding his horse in good hands. So, nervous ladies, keep an eye on your coachmen, and never insult their dignity, as we did awfully once, by doubting if a tiny infant, apparently of the tender age of five years, were sufficiently skilful to drive us over a remarkably precipitous road; and who, in consequence, jumping up and seizing the reins with lofty energy, made the pony rush up and down hill at a rate which left us breathless for several stages, and proved most positively the truth of the statistic, that the Norwegians are accustomed to driving from their infancy. Fortunately the former little runagate did not belong to the last stage, where, seated in a particularly gimcrack "*reise kjerre*," whose smart painted bars were so select in number as to allow our umbrellas to slip between their wide distances, we having neglected to strap them with the other things (which error, traveller, you must wisely avoid), had to wait an hour and a half while the "Skyd" ran back to recover them, palpitating with hopes and fears; for, were he not successful, how were such articles of luxury to be replaced? But he did find them, and we were not forced to return to Christiania at least. This delay made another stage impossible that evening, and, in consequence, we were obliged to stop at "Toftemoen" station, which turned out one

of the pleasantest and most original of all—
thank you for it, gimcrack car.

A landlord (great rarity) was visible; and,
seeing me cast longing looks upon a flock of
geese running about on the green, said gallantly, "You may have one if you can catch
it," which process was great fun, and good
exercise for the feet, as driving had been for
the arms all day. I decidedly approve of people
catching their own goose before eating it; but
how much more difficult a real than a human
goose is to catch! The fat farmer stood laughing at the chase, and, pronouncing the caught
animal the finest of the flock, was entrapped
into offering to pluck it.

What a pleasant thing it is not to know
Norwegian thoroughly! Else how uninteresting to have nothing to do but order what one
wants, without the thousand little explana-
tions and mistakes, blandishments and strok-
ing-down of the peasantry, which make one
feel quite friendly with them at once! Also the
study of the conversation-book, brought out
in the old hall of a night, and the recitations

therefrom before an audience, form, with the combined teaching and laughing, a complete evening's amusement.

This station had great exterior pretensions to regularity of architecture; being a long wooden building of two stories high, with the windows all at equal distances; the whole edifice raised on a mound and keeping very much out of sight the innumerable smaller constructions which dot about a Norwegian farm. Inside, in the travellers' rooms, the rough beams of the wall were covered with light-blue paint; and though the showy windows did not open, a thorough draught was kept up by none of the doors shutting; while a look of comfort was shed around by the sight of large bear-skin cloaks hanging up ready for winter. The master was, that *rara avis* in Norway, a bachelor; the peasants, generally, only waiting for a house, to marry immediately, when they are called a "husebonde;" from which our word husband (they say) is derived.

Besides the geese upon the green, there was a goodly crop of mushrooms waiting to be picked for sauce; the whole thing being too good for supper, was postponed till dinner next day, and, seeing twilight coming on, we went in to bacon instead. That taking some time to despatch, I naturally concluded afterwards, it was night outside, but found it no darker than it was an hour ago; and this is a Norwegian peculiarity the traveller must bear in mind, as at first he will often pull up his horse, thinking the coming darkness must soon prevent his proceeding any further, while in reality the short night will not begin for some hours after, and in the hot summer the pleasantest time for driving is the gloaming evening, the softened atmosphere then shedding lovely hues around. I was much struck by the twilight scene that evening; it had been a lovely day: the river behind the farm was crossed by a bridge of curious Norwegian structure, in which large pieces of unhewn wood, placed triangularly together, were heaped up till they reached and supported the planks laid across them, their roughness giving an appearance of want of perpendicular, as if one touch of a tiny pony's hoof would overbalance the whole thing: this picturesque object was in the foreground; hills of delicate colour succeeded one another into the far distance; the trees lay hid in deep-blue tones; the only sound was now and then of a fish turning in the waters. It was ten o'clock at night; I was standing in wild Norway——how many young ladies in towns were hearing the street organs play "La donna è mobile" for the six-thousandth time!

The next morning passed most pleasantly in fishing for breakfast, and afterwards sketching the imposing edifice on the hill opposite; which, painted rich crimson and divided by white pillars, had a grand effect from the valley below, and looked as if the proprietor must own all the country round. The house belonged to the brother of our landlord; a nearer approach showed the constructing material to be wood. The interior contained some slight attempts at furniture, with a few armchairs and large chests; but the wonder of the neighbourhood were several panels let into the walls, on which the proprietor and his brother had, in their boyish days, painted some mythological animals, such an accomplishment being of most uncommon occurrence; the farmer's sole library, picture, and model gallery being generally comprised in the family Bible with frontispiece of Adam and Eve. That is very likely the reason their ways are still as simple as in patriarchal times, occasionally distressingly so to those who have had the misfortune to study more worldly literature.

The farm buildings were not particularly picturesque, except where blooming shrubs growing on the roofs gave them the appearance of top-heavy flower-pots. The slanting wooden roads, by which the horses draw the hay-carts to the upper stories of the barns, were also rather pretty subjects for a sketch. The farmer had one or two friends in to see him as they drove past to Trondhjem, and he brought out some of the Madeira which had been got for the crown prince in his late journey through the land. Such nectar I have rarely tasted: the English must be under some strange delusion as

to what the real flavour of that wine is, or the
Norwegians trade direct with Spain and have
not yet learned to poison the drinking-cup.
When each had taken a glass of the exquisite
liquor, without seeming to think it out of the
common way, the farmer poured the rest into
a smaller bottle, and politely presented it to us
for our journey.

To enter into the spirit of peasant life is what
is required to fully enjoy a Norwegian excursion, and give it a peculiar character different
to all other journeys. There is no gentry in the
country, and, except in the mining districts
and widely-scattered towns, but one class of
inhabitants,—the rural. The traveller must
either then pass sulkily along, or associate with
them, who, though simple, are thoroughly well-
bred, and from whom the most refined person
need not fear to receive the slightest rudeness.
When some Yorkshire-men from '*Ull*, as they
announced themselves, came late into the hall,
and noisily ordered horses to be ready at three
o'clock the next morning to take them quickly
on, not finding anything worth staying for in

the country, I could not help thinking it would have been worth their while sparing a little time to contemplate the dignified, unselfish manner of the Norwegian peasant, which would be quite worthy of a journey to learn, even were it on arid ground, instead of amid some of the world's finest scenery.

## The Dovre-fjeld—A Fine Farm and Old Lady—Wolves—Choose your Road

Leaving Toftemoen with regret, after a few days' delightful visit and plenty of occupation for pencil and fishing-rod, we drove north-wards; the aspect of the country gradually changing with the receding valley; and as we ascended higher and higher, leaving all trees beneath, suddenly emerged on the edge of a wild plateau; that peculiar feature of Scandinavia, there called a fjeld. Dull lakes and pools of water were imbedded in grassy banks; the road, flat for the first time, wound among them and innumerable little hillocks, until, taking a sudden rise, a chain of mountains appeared in front—that noble ridge of the Dovre which cuts through Norway, and includes Schneehätten.

At the doorway of a large farmhouse, on a slope at the foot of the mountains, stood a portly lady with cheerful smile ready to welcome the new-comers, which is seldom the case in Norway; the doors of every place being left wide open, the traveller can walk in and take possession without encountering a soul, which often gives a dullness to the arrival at a strange spot, till he has become courageous in the ways of the country. The dress of this fine old lady was our first specimen of uncommon costume, and as such minutely inspected and sketched on the spot; which so delighted her that the following day, when I was sitting quietly mending my clothes, she pounced upon me, took me off to an enormous room where the family wardrobe was kept, and, selecting the best of everything, dressed me up as a Dovre-fjeld peasant for the day; presenting her handiwork with great satisfaction to all new-comers, and insisting on another drawing being made.

The whole road from Christiania to Trondhjem rings with the praises of Madame Jerkin: hers is the favourite station, to which the knowing traveller always presses on. There, though white bread is unknown, the charming light waffle-kacker are cooked in little moulds fresh for him; the cream is too thick to pour, and must be ladled out with a spoon; the floors are scrubbed now and then, and the best brandiviin from Trondhjem is kept in a corner of the cupboard. Twenty horses wait in the stable, forty cows graze on the surrounding hills in summer, and lie on Iceland moss in their stalls in winter. The flad-bröd is piled up till it touch the ceiling in the store-room; and rows of salted mutton show that meat *can* be had in an extremity. Descendants of the old kings of Norway, the Jerkin family live in good style; and if any proof of their antiquity were wanting, the lock on the barn will be found on examination to be the facsimile of the ancient one in the museum of relics in Christiania. The family consisted of Madame Jerkin, her son and his wife, grandson, and an expected baby; who must be born by this time, and have worn the extraordinary pieces of small finery made upon the model of its granny's, which were ready prepared in waiting in the wardrobe, where its mother's wadded petticoats and furred winter polkas were kept. I wish the event and christening had come off while we were in that part of the country: I am sure there would have been jolly doings, judging by the butter already prepared, and made into enormous globes resting on gaily painted stands.

The summer had been so unusually cold, that the first crop of hay only was being cut; nine mowers were at work all morning beneath the windows, and at midday came in to a dinner composed of a slice of sausage and one of cheese, and laid on a circle of flad-bröd as a plate for each person; which they ate, seated on a form fixed in the floor alongside of a table. Supper was of Gröd, or porridge, of which a large bowl stood in the centre, and another of sour cream, each dipping his spoon in succession into first one, then the other.

Sunday was marked by every one being in their best, and the porridge made of cream instead of water; it was very amusing to see it taken out of the large caldron, and the joy of the lucky being who secured the fork and the remains adhering thereto. These cross-shaped forks, the decorated salt-boxes, and the painted wooden drinking-cups, are the most remarkable domestic utensils in a Norwegian household. Going to church was out of the question; the nearest was thirty miles off, with service only once a month. The poor priest came to rest his horse in the evening at Jerkin, having still further to go home next morning, and said his life was a perpetual scene of travelling between the four distant churches, all nearly forty miles from each other, which formed his charge. To drive between them in winter must be a shuddering undertaking in such a cold, wolfy country; six animals of that tribe had only a few weeks since come down to attack the grazing cows of the farm; but, being great cowards in summer, the cries of the herd-boys kept them off their prey until assistance came from the house. This anecdote considerably damped the ardour with which we had been contemplating an expedition to the foot of Schneehätten; for though the peasants vowed no wolf would attack a human being in summer, the idea of them being all about, gave a disagreeably zoological sensation to the stranger; and—who knows—they might not make an exception to their rule in favour of ladies?

These doubts, the screams of an eagle, and the awful appearance of the mountain (curved in the centre, with overhanging rocks), made our hearts quail somewhat; and having looked up from the base to the summit of the giant, turned homewards, and were very much cheered by the sight of the high road two miles off, from whence the mountain, lately so grim, had a most charming effect, the clear northern atmosphere bathing the whole in blue, the snow of a light, the rocks of a dark shade, harmoniously combining. The peaks of other lofty mountains were also visible, nearly as high as Schneehätten, which prevent an extended view from its summit, and make the ascent desirable only to those who go for the pure love of mountain-climbing.

Returning to the farm, the sounds of merry music rang through the air, and looking above, beneath, around, to see whence they proceeded, a row of smiling faces at the upper story of a barn, said plainly, "There is fun going on here; come up." The ascent was partly by ladder and partly by pulls, but worth the trouble, for there were the maidens dancing in that graceful attitude caught by Tidemand, the national painter, when adorning the walls of the crown prince's rustic palace with scenes from the life of a peasant. Sliding along, her hair often waving from beneath her head-dress, the girl follows her partner round the room till she catches his extended hand; they then join in the lively "polztanz" together; separating afterwards, except by the one hand, she turns beneath his raised arm with a charming movement, and then goes off with him again doubly quick in the "springarbó." After each dance, the men, walking round with their partners, laid a small coin before the musician; so there was no difficulty as to who was to pay the piper. This is the Norwegian peasants' way of spending Sunday afternoon, when they can manage it. Other evenings, the tired labourers would cluster round the hearth, and listen to some musical sprite among them playing the national airs on flute or violin, joining in by voice with the more familiar ones, and singing the fine old melody, "Sons of Norway," with heartfelt enthusiasm. The first verse will be a specimen of the Norske language.

> "Sönner af Norges, det aeldgande Rige,
> Sjunger til Harpens den festlige Klang!
> Mandigt og höitids fuldt Tönen lad stige;
> Faedrene landet indvies vor Sang!
> Faedreneminder, herligt oprinder,
> Hvergang vi naevne vor Faedrene stavn;
> Svulmende Hjerten og, glödende Kinder,
> Hylde det elskte det hellige Navn."

Those were happy hours, and it was fortunate we had come in time for them; a few days later a

party of English arrived, who quite annihilated
these merry meetings. They were fine people,
who had come to Norway for salmon-fishing,
and for nothing else, and had been staying
with some friends who had their own stand,
on their own river, up in the north. The principal person was a rather fast lady, who could
drive 120 miles at once, all day and all night.
She was attended by several sportsmen, who
were not inclined to be civil to other travellers;
and we had the pleasure of seeing the principal
London newspapers arrive, be read, and pock-
eted, without the chance of a peep at one in
that far-distant region. The singing circle was
broken up, and the peasants seated round the
walls of the room instead, while the exclusive
party's table was drawn before the fire; and
one evening there was a most amusing row,
occasioned by Madame Jerkin, after they had
been about an hour at tea, slily slipping the
pot off the table, and with a wink giving two
Norwegian ladies, who had arrived cold and
late, a cup out of it; which being discovered,
ferocious cries of "Where's the teapot?" echoed

through the hall; and the interpreter, or *Tolk* (as they disdained personal communication with the people), was summoned to give a good lecture to the offender. The peasants took all this in perfect quiet, but when they left, charged them just double what they did us and other travellers; and this is an example of how every country which the British frequent, gradually changes both its character and prices. Tolks, or interpreters, a mild sort of courier, were never heard of some years ago, and are most absurd appendages in a country where travellers must either sit in the kitchen or in their own bedrooms. This party did nothing but smoke large tobacco-pipes all day; and though each had a trunk behind his carriole, besides a common luggage-cart, were in a jagged state of attire; not the least picturesque, but with a forlorn "Jeremy Diddler" effect. Fortunately an agreeable and talented English artist, who came to study stags, and his companion, a member of the Royal Society, had preceded this Mayfair party on the same road, and, staying some time, produced a favourable impression of English sense, not likely to be effaced immediately; so a young native engineer told me who was making plans for a new road to Trondhjem. The crown prince had noticed on his journey how suddenly the road mounted at Jerkin (the stations have the same names as their proprietors), and he soon after sent a competent person to plan one, which, by making a sweep of several miles, would be less abrupt.

It was hard to say farewell to this spot; the constant arrival of travellers made it a most amusing station, and showed the ways of the travelling natives, who were all frank, easy, and delighted to give information: sometimes Norwegian ladies would drive up in yellow waterproof cloaks and hoods, and grey "uglies." The neighbouring lake and stream had plenty of excellent fish, which was proved one day by forty trout being caught by a line made of a string attached to a young tree; and as for game, some sportsmen bagged a score of ptarmigan, or *Ryper*, in one morning, of delicious quality. A Norwegian gentleman was going the same way, and, tearing ourselves from good Madame Jerkin, we drove rapidly down to the fjeld again.

Now, traveller, before turning with us, you must consider your plans and your map. The usual route for the English is to continue straight on to Trondhjem, take the steamer there, and coast round to Christiania again— quite plain sailing, but you will have no real idea what Norway is. The great beauties of the road terminate at the Dovre-fjeld; from the summit you will have had a good idea of the stern character of the scenery further on. At Trondhjem, the only remarkable object is a church, thought a wonder from being of stone instead of wood, otherwise common-place enough; whereas, if you take the westward course, you will have plenty of novelty and hardships; and as you must be a little initiated into the style of country by this time, you will not be more nervous than we were, in pene-trating into wilds where English ladies had never been heard of, and only one Norwegian lady had once given the inhabitants an idea of the refined feminine world beyond.

# A CRUISE ON THE HARDANGER FIORD

*or,*
*Six in Norway with a "Snark",*
*by One of Them*

## BY EDWARD STANFORD,
## JUNIOR, 1881

A hand-written inscription on The London Library's copy of this rare pamphlet reveals the author as EDWARD STANFORD, JUNIOR, son of the founder of the great travel bookseller and publisher Stanfords. Stanford travelled to Norway when he was twenty-five and later took over the family business. Notable personalities such as Florence Nightingale, Ernest Shackleton and Dr Watson (in *The Hound of the Baskervilles*) visited the shop. Edward Stanford, Junior died in 1917.

*Dedicated*
*Without Permission*
*to:*

| | |
|---|---|
| THE COMMODORE | FRED SCRUTTON. |
| THE CAPTAIN | A. J. R. MEREDITH. |
| THE PURSER | J. HERBERT SCRUTTON. |
| THE JESTER | HERBERT J. BARROW. |
| THE MUSICIAN | PERCY E. SCRUTTON. |

BY

| | |
|---|---|
| THE INTERPRETER | EDWARD STANFORD, JUN. |

**C**amping out on the Thames becomes daily a greater impossibility, and pastures new have to be sought by those who love open-air life and water scenery. Perhaps some of our friends will like to hear of some experiences of a new happy hunting-ground, with the advantages of accessibility, freedom, foreign travel, grand scenery, and, last but not least, comparative cheapness.

Those who are well acquainted with the Hardanger Fiord had better leave the following account unread. I have nothing new to tell them. My only wish is to give such details from personal experience as would be useful to any one who has not visited the district, but who may be looking out for something novel in the way of a boating holiday. I must further apologise for the diary form adopted; but this style, so awkward to handle, is the only one which allows the day-by-day variety of the trip to appear—a variety which constitutes the chief charm of the life; and if any gentlemen are induced to follow in our footsteps, may they be as lucky as we were.

Our party consisted of six, whom I shall call after their principal functions, Commodore, Captain, Purser, Jester, Musician, and Interpreter, the last being named on the *lucus a non lucendo* principle: he merely possessed a dictionary. The Commodore had previously visited the fiord in his canoe, so he and the Captain designed a boat, which was eventually built by Messrs. Forrestt, and christened the "Snark." She was a four-oared double-ended whaling gig, built of pine and mahogany, fitted with a centre-board, two masts, balance lug-sails, and foresail; dimensions twenty-two feet long, five feet three inches beam, two feet deep amidships. Many and diverse were the opinions expressed before all things were ready; the condensation of a month's necessaries, including air bed and heavy boots, into a kit of thirty lbs. was a problem; and on the question of supply our two cooks disagreed. At length, however, the meats, soups, jams, &c., were packed in four boxes, made to fit in the bottom of the boat where they served as ballast, and we found ourselves early in June the centre of some interest and more luggage at King's Cross station.

Our intention was to go by steamer to Bergen *viâ* Hull, launch the "Snark," and coast southwards through the islands until we came to the Hardanger, where we expected to spend a month. We were to camp out when it suited us—i.e., when there was no good "station" (inn), or when the scenery and weather were tempting. We expected to be obliged to camp in the barren rocky stretch of islands below Bergen, and for this purpose we took two tents of oiled sheeting, each seven feet high, nine feet long, and eight feet wide. I now think it is possible to do the trip without any camping, a course which would perhaps lessen expense and labour, but would destroy much fun and freedom.

I pass over the horrors of Hull and the details of our life on board the Wilson steamship "Domino." Suffice it that the passengers took much interest in our movements, and the crew of the "Snark" began to exhibit a certain easy unconventionality which developed itself alarmingly before our return. In about forty hours from Hull, we reached the port of Stavanger, and our "experiences" began. The captain of the "Domino" kindly volunteered to drop us at Moster, the mouth of the Hardanger, and thus save us the roughest and most uninteresting piece of work, if we could get our provisions cleared by the Customs at Stavanger. Custom House officials seem cast in one mould all over the world. The ceremony of examination was finished in an hour; but the steamer was waiting and whistling for us as we pulled back across the harbour, murmuring many quaint blessings on the advantages of protection. We had been fleeced of 3*l*. odd for duty on our stores, and had made a careful study of many departments.

The next few hours were spent in macintoshes preparing for the drop-overboard. Our Musician shed tobacco from the skirts of his clothing as he went down the ship's side, but the wary Custom House officers, who had popped out like spiders to meet us, did not notice it, and we parted with tossed oars, three hearty cheers for the Captain, and an enlivening tootle on the post horn. At Moster we had our first taste of a Norwegian "station"—i.e., bare bed-rooms and plain wholesome living—but were very pleased with everything except flad-bröd, the bread of the country, a thin wafer-like substance resembling crisp brown paper intermingled with blotting, sawdust, and straw. It is doubtless very nourishing, and suitable for the people, like oatmeal for the Scotch; but the taste for it must be acquired. We saw piles of it packed from floor to ceiling in several houses. Moral, take biscuits!

From Moster we sailed all day, passing through the strait at Herö, and on to the station at Dimmelsvik. The weather was bad and the wind squally, but we were quite satisfied with our first experience of the "Snark" in open water.

The next day we sailed on to Aakrehaven on the large island Varaldsö—a lovely spot with wild lilies of the valley in blossom on the rocks—and then on to near Griotnaes, where we camped in a pine wood at the top of a boggy slope. In the evening we made a roaring fire of pine branches, and sat round, singing songs to the banjo, after watching the pink tints fade away slowly from the snow on the opposite hills. But next morning a change came o'er the spirit of the scene. An ominous patter was heard on our tents, and breakfast had to be cooked under many difficulties. Packing up also was unpleasant, and after launching and trying a couple of tacks, we had recourse to our oars. A very hard pull through a choppy sea in pouring rain brought us to Jondal, a station which will ever be gratefully remembered. We had been working hard for eight or nine hours without food, but after changing our clothes, our hostess set such a dinner for hungry men before us that the morning's experiences vanished from our minds. Baedeker says Jondal is famous for its boats, and certainly the natives seemed much interested in our specimen of English work. Throughout the whole expedition the "Snark" was always a centre of interest—almost an introduction—and when she had to be beached or launched, hands were always found ready and willing to help us.

The next day was spent in a walk up the valley, and a stiff climb up a hill to the south, from the top of which a splendid panorama of snow mountain and fiord opened out to our view. Here we crossed our first snow, and saw a white hare. On the way home a woman gave us some milk, in a curious bowl surrounded with English verses. How it reached that out-of-the-way spot was a riddle.

We sailed next morning from Jondal, after much hand-shaking—a very pleasing feature of Norwegian life. When you leave a station, your host and hostess shake you by the hand, wishing you a happy journey; and if you give anything to a Norwegian (old meat tins are always thankfully received), he will give your hand a silent grip more expressive than many words. The wind soon dropped, and we pulled into the charming bay of Noreimsund. Here we landed and walked up to the Oosthusfos, a small but pretty fall of 150 feet, with a path running between the water and the rock over which it leaps. From Noreim, a couple of hours' pull brought us to a lovely spot on the east shore of the Fiksensund, and we pitched our tents on a little wooded slope under an almost perpendicular cliff. The evening was perfect; the tints of the hills opposite at Samlenaes, if painted, would have been pronounced impossible, and we sat round our fire until the moon sent a silver streak right across the fiord to where the waves were lapping lazily round the "Snark."

Next morning, after breakfasting on fish we had seen caught, we left our impedimenta in the tents, and started in a light boat to explore the Fiksensund, to my mind the most beautiful of the arms of the Hardanger. The sun shone hot and bright as we sailed slowly down the very narrow sound with dozens of waterfalls trickling down its wooded precipices. Occasionally a porpoise would show

his black fin, or a fish splash, but otherwise
the scene was perfect peace, except when
we roused threefold or fourfold echoes with
our horn. That afternoon we tried to beat
onwards, but soon took to our oars, and after
a hard pull through lumpy water, we camped
at Gravene. Next morning, after a cow had
brought one tent down on us by her experi-
ments with the supports, we received a visit
from a Norwegian, at whose wedding our
Commodore had "assisted" some three years
before. A very cordial invitation followed, and
led to our calling at his house, and being hos-
pitably entertained.

At Utne we found the nicest station on the
fiord. Our landlady, Mme. Utne, a splendid
old picture of eighty, was an old friend of the
Commodore, and took us all under her hospitable wings, as if we were members of her family.
In the evening we sat in a dry barge off the
pierhead, and sang all our songs for the benefit
of a large Norse audience. We presume they
were pleased, because next morning a letter
was found on our doorstep thanking us for our

"beautiful sing" (Heaven save the mark!), and signed, "A young boy from Norway!" That day a confirmation was being held at Kinservik, four miles across the fiord, so of course we went, like the rest of the district, in our own boat. The church was so full that we could scarcely enter the porch. We counted more than a hundred boats, besides a large steamer from Odde, and we estimated over a thousand people were there. A large circle of spectators surrounded us everywhere; but we were by this time tolerably used to being stared at, and we had a splendid opportunity of studying the costumes and physiognomy of the district. The former are decidedly picturesque, but each district has its own peculiarity. On the Hardanger the women wear scarlet bodices and white caps with large projecting flaps, something like elephant's ears. The hair is generally braided in two pigtails, which are tied together with ribbons at the end. In feature the women are often very good-looking, with clear ruddy complexions, bright blue eyes, and light hair, and the children are generally pictures. After the confirmation was over, Mme. Utne consented to honour our boat, and a most exciting race commenced between the "Snark" and the native boats. A four miles' course in pouring rain at top speed is calculated to try one's training, but the "Snark" reached home first by about one hundred and fifty yards. The native boats are generally made of six planks, and are very picturesque, on account of their high double ends. They are light and well adapted for the waters; but good oars and rowlocks would render them twice as effective.

The next day, after cheers for Mme. Utne, we pulled away steadily nearly all day to Tyssedal, three miles from the end of the Sör Fiord, and pitched our tents on a little height on the edge of a pine wood, with the roar of a torrent in our ears, the fiord at our feet, and snow mountains rising straight out of the water beyond.

Next morning we started inland, with our Commodore as guide, for the Skjaeggedalsfos, a waterfall of 530 feet clear leap, which

Baedeker calls "stupendous" and "overwhelmingly grand." After about two hours and a half along a very rough path, we came to a farm and large lake 1500 feet above the sea. It took two men one hour and a half to row us up the lake. We could not have seen the fall under more favourable auspices. The weather was hot, and as it was early in the summer, the volume of water was very large. The winter, however, had been unusually severe and late, so that the huge cataract disappeared into an enormous snow bed, and emerged some quarter of a mile lower down, carrying lumps of ice far out into the lake. A very rough scramble on our hands and knees brought us almost under the fall, so that, looking up, it seemed as if the enormous cloud of soft white spray must descend and bury us. At other times rockets of molten glass would seem to shoot out from the fleecy clouds, and rainbow tints flickered about in all directions. The effect was indeed stupendous, much more striking than the better-known Vöringsfos which we visited later. The position of the fall amid bare mountains is unique, and no one is likely to forget his first glimpse of the huge fall descending from the sky line down a naked precipice at the end of a lake of indescribable colour and clearness. On our return we partook of vile coffee, fair milk, and bad flad-bröd at the farm. The pleasure of the excursion is much spoilt by the presence of a sort of Caliban who lives at the farm, and acts as boatman and interpreter. The Norwegian Tourist Club has done so much for the path up to the farm that I should suggest its doing a little more. A small pension conditional on Caliban's removal elsewhere would be money well spent.

The same evening we pulled into Odde, whence we made the first ascent that year of the Folgefond—a huge plateau of snow and ice, which forms a striking feature in many Hardanger landscapes. From this plateau glaciers descend towards the fiord; the two best known are the Buarbrae near Odde, and the Bondhusbrae, on the west side of the ridge, both very picturesque, and only about 1,000 feet above water level. The Buarbrae has been

rapidly advancing of late years. We started
from Odde at 6.20 a.m., and in about two
hours reached the foot of the glacier. Our guide
then took us up a steep hill to the right, and
after a hard climb we looked down on the blue
glacier, and a tarn still covered with ice. We
lunched on the last bare rocks, and then began
a tiring climb over soft snow, until we reached
a ridge whence we could see nothing but snow
around us, the fiord seawards, and the hilltops
to the east, the only striking feature of which
was the mountain of Haarteigen, a truncated
cone 5,550 feet high, which seemed to stand
alone in solitary blackness. The descent was
monotonous until we reached some nice snow
slopes, where glissading races were the order
of the day. The guide said he had never seen
the snow so low as on that 16th of June. The
Buarbrae is a very pretty glacier, and well
worth a climb; but a simple walk across the
Folgefond entails much labour, and at the end
one feels inclined to give Mr. Punch's cele-
brated advice, "Don't." Before the evening of
the next day we had pulled on to Ullensvang,

where we cooked supper, and then sailed on all night up the Eidfiord, reaching Vik in due course. A night in a twenty-two-feet open boat, with five other fellows, mostly over six feet long, with their stores and luggage, is not my idea of luxury or rest, but the fiat went forth, and we suffered accordingly.

The weather was piping hot, and the nights are almost as light as the days, but we duly appreciated our beds at the very dear station of Vik, the only one on the Hardanger considered by us and the guidebooks unreasonable in its charges. Probably the very fine and accessible waterfall of the Vöringsfos is to blame. The Tourist Club has made a capital path up the grand ravine through which the torrent from the fall rushes, and the maintenance of this path is charged in each person's bill; but it would seem impossible to see the fall itself well, because of the drenching, blinding spray. At our visit the quantity of water was very great; perhaps later one can see more, but we could scarcely open our eyes when we came close to the fall. The actual plunge of the water struck me as finer than that of the Skjaeggedalsfos, but the chasm and the surroundings are not so grand. At the Skjaeggedalsfos one feels alone with Nature— as it were, in her own chosen haunt— but there is an air of civilisation, not to say of the theatre, about the Vöringsfos which renders the excursion less enjoyable; and the bill at the station on your return adds to the impression. That evening we camped at the mouth of the Osa Fiord, where we enjoyed some good sailing, and once ran considerable risk of a capsize. A sudden squall swept down a gully with great force, and the whole crew had to sit upon the gunwale. From this camp we revisited our kind friends at Utne, and then on to Eide. Here we left our boat and walked inland northwards to Gudvangen and the Sogne Fiord, *viâ* Vossevangen, a hundred miles there and back. This splendid excursion well repays you for the time and trouble spent; the Naero Valley, near Gudvangen, surpasses anything I have seen in Scotland or the Tyrol. But as this district is off the fiord, I must refer inquirers to the guidebooks. From Eide to Jondal, and Jondal to Aenaes, were the last stages in the "Snark," our little craft beating in to the last-named place in perfect style. We spent two nights here under canvas, and, after visiting the Bondhus Glacier, were carried back to Bergen by steamer. I should like to record here the great courtesy and kindness of the captain, who refused all remuneration for carrying our boat.

To sum up, then, the results of our trip. We travelled 136 miles by oars and 118 by sail; we were absent thirty-three days; we camped out ten times, and slept (?) once in the boat; and our expenses came to about 30*l.* apiece, including boat, tents, &c., and other property, which, by the brilliant auctioneering skill of our Purser, fetched very good prices later.

Careful seamanship in squally mountain waters is a *sine quâ non*, but with that the trip ought to be accomplished without accident. The winds are, however, variable and shifty, so that a sailing boat pure and simple might take a long time reaching Odde, and a rowing boat of a size calculated to stand the sea is not always a pleasure to pull in lumpy water. A crew of six young fellows who will work well together for a month is difficult to make up, especially when two at least must be used to navigating a sailing boat, and the rest be all-round hands who can be relied upon to work when work has to be done. Shirking or selfishness would ruin such a party, and there is generally enough work for the day. A musician is a great acquisition and help with the natives, who are very simple-minded, and willing to be amused. In Norway life is not regulated on our English catch-a-train principles; but with a good-humoured, pleasant bearing, and patience, a trip of this kind may be a source of the greatest pleasure——the delightful memory of past experiences.

## Mem. as to "Snarks"

For information as to the exact nature of a "Snark," I would refer the inquiring student to Mr. Lewis Carroll's delightful work on the subject; but for the benefit of those who have not the time to make independent researches in such abstruse regions of natural history, I will add the concise and conclusive opinion of an acquaintance of mine when that Great Treatise first appeared. A "Snark" is a female "Boojum," and a "Boojum" is a male "Snark." *Verb. sap*. The word has such a distinctly Norse flavour about it, that the very name of our beautiful little craft added something to our popularity on the Hardanger Fiord.

PUSHKIN PRESS—THE LONDON LIBRARY

## "FOUND ON THE SHELVES"

THE LONDON LIBRARY (a registered charity) is one of the UK's leading literary institutions and a favourite haunt of authors, researchers and keen readers.

Membership is open to all.

Join at www.londonlibrary.co.uk.

www.pushkinpress.com